JUL   2010

GRAPHIC LIBRARY™

GRAPHIC SCIENCE

THE SURPRISING WORLD OF BACTERIA

with MAX AXIOM SUPER SCIENTIST

by Agnieszka Biskup

illustrated by Tod G. Smith

Consultant:
Dr. Beth Traxler
Associate Professor of Microbiology
University of Washington
Seattle, Washington

CAPSTONE PRESS
a capstone imprint

Graphic Library is published by Capstone Press,
151 Good Counsel Drive, P.O. Box 669, Mankato, Minnesota 56002.
www.capstonepress.com

092009
005619WZS10

 Books published by Capstone Press are manufactured with paper
containing at least 10 percent post-consumer waste.

Library of Congress Cataloging-in-Publication Data
Biskup, Agnieszka.
  The surprising world of bacteria with Max Axiom, super scientist / by Agnieszka
Biskup ; illustrated by Tod G. Smith and Anne Timmons.
    p. cm. — (Graphic library. Graphic science)
  Summary: "In graphic novel format, follows Max Axiom as he explores the world of
bacteria" — Provided by publisher.
  Includes bibliographical references and index.
  ISBN 978-1-4296-3975-0 (library binding)
  ISBN 978-1-4296-4863-9 (paperback)
  1. Bacteria — Comic books, strips, etc. — Juvenile literature. I. Smith, Tod, ill.
II. Timmons, Anne, ill. III. Title.
QR74.8.B57 2010
579.3 — dc22   2009035303

Designer	*Media Researcher*
Alison Thiele	Wanda Winch
Cover Colorist	*Production Specialist*
Krista Ward	Laura Manthe
Colorist	*Editor*
Matt Webb	Anthony Wacholtz

Photo illustration credits: AVRDC - The World Vegetable Center, 19; Shutterstock/
Sebastian Kaulitzki, 9

TABLE OF CONTENTS

5

Bacteria are survivors. Some types of bacteria can thrive where no other living things are found.

Some bacteria live in the extremely salty waters of the Dead Sea.

Bacteria have been found deep under Antarctic ice.

They live in near-boiling temperatures at the hot springs of Yellowstone National Park.

Bacteria have even been found in clouds high above earth's surface.

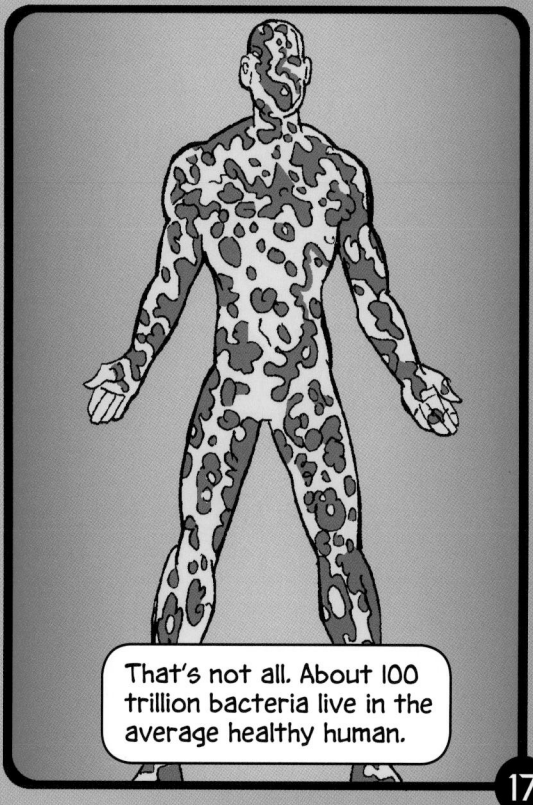

That's not all. About 100 trillion bacteria live in the average healthy human.

But I also saw some bacteria that were harmful.

That's true. Bacteria that cause diseases are called pathogenic.

They're responsible for several illnesses, including food poisoning, strep throat, and the bubonic plague.

Luckily, our bodies have a defense system against bad bacteria.

I'm going to shrink back down to take a closer look at how our bodies fight back.

BAD BACTERIA

ACCESS GRANTED: MAX AXIOM

Pathogenic bacteria can attack plants, animals, fungi, and even other bacteria. Pathogenic bacteria can create holes in leaves by releasing toxins that damage cells.

19

Some giant bacteria are 1,000 times larger than normal bacteria. One, called *Epulopiscium fischelsoni*, is found in the intestines of surgeonfish. It's so big, it can be seen with the naked eye.

Anaerobic bacteria don't need oxygen to live. Anaerobic bacteria live in soil and even inside our bodies. They're mostly harmless. But if they travel to a part of the body where they don't belong, they can cause serious illness and disease.

In 1928, Alexander Fleming discovered that a type of common mold could kill pathogenic bacteria. He isolated the bacteria-killing chemical from the mold and called it penicillin. It was the first antibiotic ever discovered.

Bacteria that live in the stomachs of cows and other cud-chewing animals help them digest tough plants and grasses.

Botulinum toxin, a poison produced by *Clostridium botulinum* bacteria, is one of the most deadly naturally occurring substances known. Despite this fact, doctors use very small amounts of the toxin to treat some medical conditions. It is best known today for its use as Botox. It is injected into the face where it paralyzes muscles, helping reduce lines and wrinkles.

Vaccines have been made for bacterial diseases such as whooping cough, diphtheria, tetanus, and Lyme disease.

E. coli move by whipping their flagella. They can travel a distance equal to 25 times their length in only a second.

 Bacteria have changed the face of the planet. About two or three billion years ago, bacteria that used sunlight for energy emerged. They also gave off oxygen in the process. Thanks to bacteria, the oxygen we depend on started appearing in earth's atmosphere.

MORE ABOUT

SUPER SCIENTIST

Real name: Maxwell J. Axiom
Hometown: Seattle, Washington
Height: 6' 1"   Weight: 192 lbs
Eyes: Brown   Hair: None

Super capabilities: Super intelligence; able to shrink to the size of an atom; sunglasses give x-ray vision; lab coat allows for travel through time and space.

Origin: Since birth, Max Axiom seemed destined for greatness. His mother, a marine biologist, taught her son about the mysteries of the sea. His father, a nuclear physicist and volunteer park ranger, schooled Max on the wonders of earth and sky.

One day on a wilderness hike, a megacharged lightning bolt struck Max with blinding fury. When he awoke, Max discovered a newfound energy and set out to learn as much about science as possible. He traveled the globe earning degrees in every aspect of the field. Upon his return, he was ready to share his knowledge and new identity with the world. He had become Max Axiom, Super Scientist.

GLOSSARY

antibiotic (an-ti-bye-OT-ik) — a drug that kills bacteria and is used to cure infections and disease

bacilli (bah-SILL-ee) — rod-shaped bacteria

binary fission (BYE-ner-ee FI-shuhn) — form of reproduction where the DNA is copied and the bacteria splits into two cells

cell (SEL) — the smallest unit of a living thing

cocci (KAH-kye) — ball-shaped bacteria

decomposer (dee-kuhm-PO-zur) — a living thing that turns dead things into food for others

DNA (dee en AY) — the genetic material that carries all of the instructions to make a living thing and keep it working; DNA stands for deoxyribonucleic acid.

eukaryotic cell (u-kare-ee-AH-tik SEL) — a cell that has DNA enclosed in a nucleus

flagellum (flah-GEL-luhm) — a whiplike tail that helps bacteria move

immune system (i-MYOON SISS-tuhm) — the part of the body that protects against germs and diseases

microorganism (mye-kroh-OR-guh-niz-uhm) — a living thing too small to be seen without a microscope

prokaryotic cell (pro-kare-ee-AH-tik SEL) — a cell that does not have a nucleus

spirilla (spuh-RILL-ah) — spiral-shaped bacteria

vaccine (vak-SEEN) — dead or weakened germs injected into a person or animal to help fight disease

READ MORE

Brunelle, Lynn, and Barbara Ravage. *Bacteria: Discovery Channel School Science*. Milwaukee, Wis.: Gareth Stevens Publishing, 2003.

Farrell, Jeanette. *Invisible Allies: Microbes That Shape Our Lives*. New York: Farrar, Straus, and Giroux, 2005.

Nye, Bill. *Bill Nye the Science Guy's Great Big Book of Tiny Germs*. New York: Hyperion Books for Children, 2005.

Romanek, Trudee. *Achoo! The Most Interesting Book You'll Ever Read About Germs*. Tonawanda, N.Y.: Kids Can Press, 2003.

Walker, Richard. *Microscopic Life*. Boston: Kingfisher, 2004.

INTERNET SITES

FactHound offers a safe, fun way to find Internet sites related to this book. All sites on FactHound have been researched by our staff.

Here's all you do:

Visit *www.facthound.com*

FactHound will fetch the best sites for you!

INDEX